# Dinosaurs

Edited by Belinda Gallagher
Cover design by Oxprint Ltd.

Published by Longmeadow Press, 201 High Ridge Road, Stamford,
CT 06904. All rights reserved. No part of this book may be
reproduced or utilized in any form or by any means,
electronic or mechanical, including photocopying, recording
or by any information storage and retrieval system, without
permission in writing from the Publisher.

Library of Congress Cataloging-in-Publication Data
ISBN: 0-681-45435-0
Printed in China
First Longmeadow Press Edition 1993
0 9 8 7 6 5 4 3 2 1

# LEARN ABOUT

# Dinosaurs

Written by Jane and David Glover
Illustrated by Brian Watson

LONGMEADOW
PRESS

The word dinosaur means 'terrible lizard'. Like lizards, snakes and turtles, dinosaurs were reptiles. Millions of years ago they were common, but now there are none left. They are extinct.

Today, the living animal most like a dinosaur is the crocodile. Like cousins, dinosaurs and crocodiles look alike in some ways but are different in others.

A crocodile's legs stick out sideways so that it walks with its body close to the ground. Dinosaurs stood with their legs underneath their bodies. Some, like the huge apatosaurus, stood on all four legs – it was a gentle plant-eater. Others, like the fierce hunter tyrannosaurus rex, stood up on their back legs.

There were many different kinds of dinosaur. But not all of them were alive at the same time. The plateosaurus and the teratosaurus were two of the first. They lived about 200 million years ago.

As time passed some kinds of dinosaur died out. New kinds took their place.

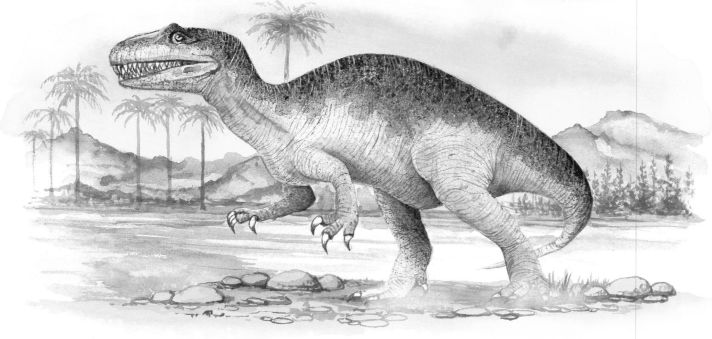

The stegosaurus lived 140 million years ago – the iguanodon 10 million years later. Triceratops and the ankylosaurus were two of the last kinds of dinosaurs on Earth. They lived 65 million years ago.

Then, suddenly, all the dinosaurs disappeared. The first men and women did not live until millions of years later. So no human being has ever seen a living dinosaur.

The dinosaurs were all land animals. They lived in the deserts, on the grasslands, in the jungle and in swamps. Their bones have been found all over the world – in America, Europe, Africa and Asia.

Triceratops lived in herds on the plains in America. They were plant-eaters and browsed on grass and shrubs. If they were

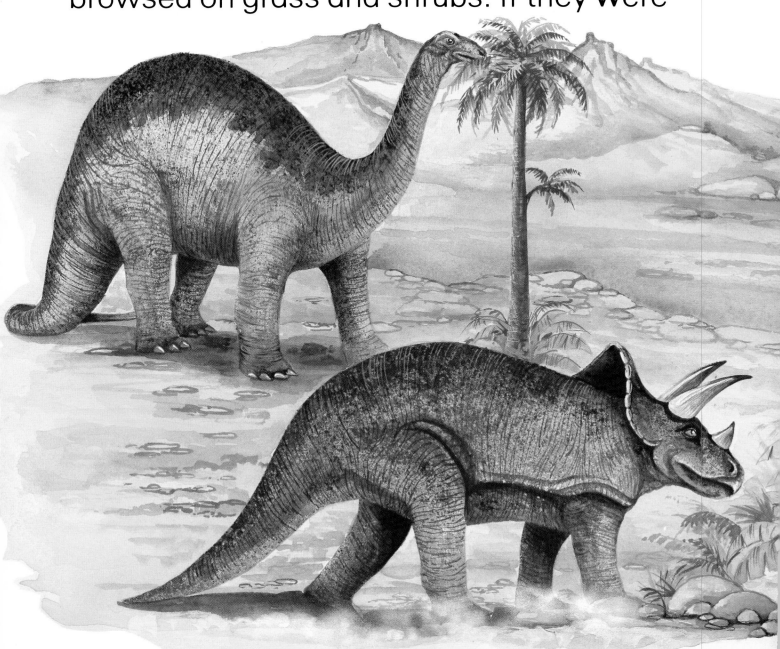

attacked by a tyrannosaurus the herd might have formed a circle and used their horns to protect the babies.

The biggest dinosaurs probably lived in swamps. The mud and water would have helped to support their heavy bodies. They used their long necks to browse on trees and water plants.

Not all dinosaurs were giants. The tiny micropachycephalosaurus was smaller than a chicken. Other dinosaurs were as big as dogs, some the size of horses, and some as big as elephants. But the biggest were really huge.

The diplodocus was the longest and the barosaurus the tallest, but the biggest

dinosaur of all was the brachiosaurus. It was heavier than 16 elephants, taller than a house and as long as three buses. It was the biggest land animal that has ever lived. The big dinosaurs had very small brains for their size. They would have moved very slowly and spent nearly all their time eating to keep their huge bodies going.

Most dinosaurs were plant-eaters. The diplodocus and the brachiosaurus were tall enough to take the leaves from the tops of trees. The iguanodon was not quite as big but it stood on its back legs to reach the lower branches and leaves. Small dinosaurs browsed on shrubs and grass at ground level. The plant-eaters were hunted by the

meat-eating dinosaurs. The allosaurus was one of the fiercest. It was 32 feet (10m) long, as heavy as an elephant and hunted the biggest plant eaters.

Deinonychus was lighter and quicker. It chased smaller prey and used the vicious claws on its back feet to stab its victims. Its name means 'terrible claw'.

Some of the plant-eaters had armour to protect their bodies from their enemies. The ankylosaurus was covered with bony plates and spikes. It could use its tail as a club to defend itself from the biggest meat eater of all – tyrannosaurus rex.

Many dinosaurs would have lived in groups for protection. Male pachycephalosauri banged their bony heads together to decide who should be leader of the herd. Mountain goats do the same thing today.

Nearly all the dinosaurs laid eggs. The protoceratops laid its eggs in a nest in the sand. The newly hatched babies would have been about the same size as rats. The parents guarded the babies from nest robbers like the velociraptor and the oviraptor.

The biggest mystery about dinosaurs is why they all suddenly died out. Scientists are still arguing about this and no one knows the real reason.

Perhaps the weather changed and it became too hot.

Maybe new plants grew with poisons that killed the plant eating dinosaurs. If all the plant-eaters died, then the meat-eaters would have died as well.

Some scientists think that dust clouds made by volcanoes or by meteorites from space might have blocked out the Sun and made the Earth much colder.
Whatever the reason there are no dinosaurs today. We have learned everything we know about them from their fossils.

Fossils are dinosaur bones and remains that have turned into rock after being buried for millions of years.

Scientists dig up the bones and put them back together like jigsaws. From their skeletons we can guess what the dinosaurs looked like when they were alive. The shape of their teeth tells us if they ate plants or meat.

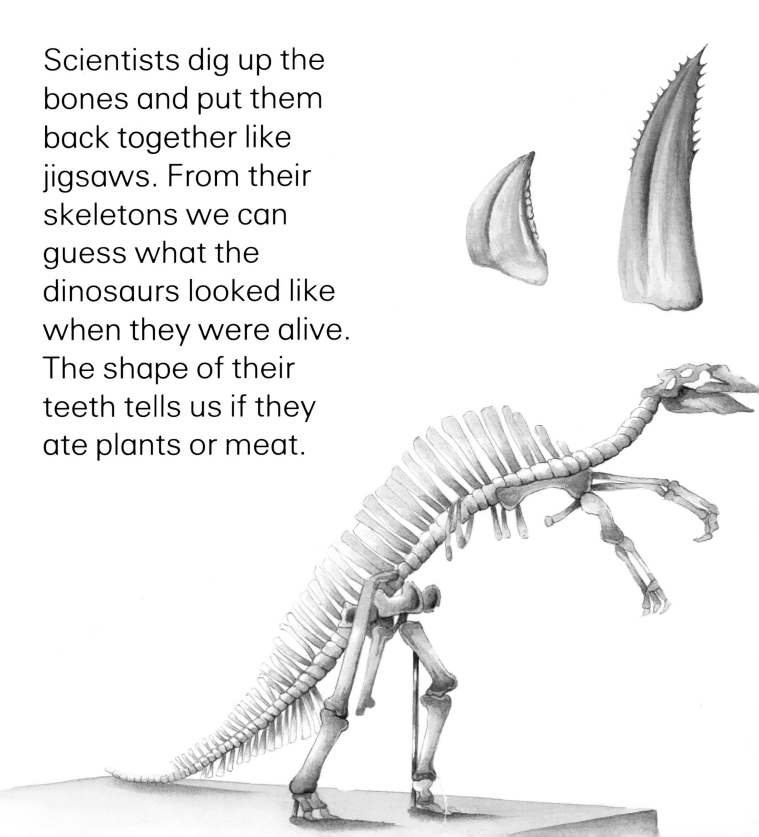

In some places, fossil footprints have been found. These show us how the dinosaurs stood and walked.

What did dinosaurs really look like? Perhaps their skins were camouflaged to hide them from their enemies. In the jungle they might have been mottled brown and green.

Dinosaurs were not the only giant reptiles to become extinct.
Plesiosaurs and ichthyosaurs swam in the seas. These died out.
Pterosaurs were flying reptiles.
The quetzalcoatlus had a wingspan of over 39 feet (12m). It was the biggest flying animal that has ever lived.

At the same time as the giant reptiles, there were small furry animals living on the ground. When the great reptiles disappeared these creatures survived. They were the ancestors of the mammals – the mice, cats, dogs, bears and monkeys – that live today. Have the dinosaurs really vanished completely? Some scientists think that their closest living relatives, closer even than crocodiles, are the birds. Perhaps the sparrows in your garden are descendants of the dinosaurs!

# Dinosaur quiz

Now that you have read about dinosaurs how many of these questions can you answer? Look back in the book for help if you need it.

## True or false?
1. Dinosaurs were reptiles.
2. Most dinosaurs laid eggs.
3. Triceratops was one of the first dinosaurs.
4. People once hunted dinosaurs for food.
5. Some dinosaurs were smaller than dogs.

## Odd one out.
Which is the odd one out and why?

6. quetzalcoatlus  ankylosaurus  iguanodon

7. diplodocus     allosaurus     brachiosaurus

8. tyrannosaurus deinonychus triceratops

# Answers

1. True
2. True
3. False – triceratops was one of the *last* dinosaurs.
4. False – the first people did not live until millions of years after the last dinosaurs.
5. True
6. Quetzalcoatlus – it was not a dinosaur. It can also fly.
7. Allosaurus – it was a meat eater, the others ate plants.
8. Triceratops – it was a plant eater, the others ate meat.